WAYS OF OVERCOMING ANXIETY:
Successful ways to fight anxiety in our lives

Dan G.Hicks

Table Of Contents

Chapter 1

Stopping overthinking

Constant worrying and overthinking may frequently lead to concerns with mental health and well-being. Techniques such as deep breathing, meditation, self-compassion, and asking for support from a healthcare professional may help ease the stress of overthinking.

Destructive thought patterns
You finally get a few peaceful minutes to yourself, only to instantly start thinking whether you forgot to send that thank-you email or if you've overstated your odds of earning the promotion.

Sound familiar? Worrying and overthinking are part of the human experience, but when left uncontrolled, they may take a toll on your well-being. Dwelling on the same ideas

may potentially raise your risk of some mental health issues.
So, what's an overthinking person to do? These recommendations might help you proceed in the correct path.

1. Step back and look at how you're reacting
The way you react to your ideas might sometimes trap you in a cycle of rumination, or recurrent thinking. Rumination may frequently create negative repercussions Trusted Source to a person's mental wellness.

The next time you find yourself repeatedly mulling things over in your head, take notice of how it impacts your mood.

Do you feel furious, anxious, or guilty? What's the fundamental feeling underlying your thoughts?

Having self-awareness is crucial to altering your thinking.

2. Find a distraction
Shut off overthinking by engaging yourself
in an activity you like.

This looks different for everyone, but
suggestions include:

learning some new cooking abilities by
tackling a new dish
going to your favorite fitness class
taking up a new pastime, such as painting
helping with a local organization
It might be hard to start anything new when
you're swamped by your ideas. If finding a
diversion seems intimidating, consider
setting aside a tiny block of time — say, 30
minutes — every other day. Use this time to
either discover possible diversions or
indulge in current ones.

3. Take a deep breath

You've heard it a million times, but that's because it works. The next time you find yourself tossing and turning over your thoughts, shut your eyes and breathe deeply.

Try it
Here's a wonderful introductory activity to help you relax with your breath:

Find a comfortable location to sit and relax your neck and shoulders.
Place one hand over your heart and the other over your tummy.

Inhale and exhale through your nose, paying attention to how your chest and stomach move as you breathe.
Try completing this exercise 3 times a day for 5 minutes, or anytime you have racing thoughts.

4. Meditate
Developing a regular meditation practice is an evidence-backed method to help clear

your mind of anxious chatter by shifting your attention inward.

All you need is 5 minutes and a calm area.

5. Look at the wider picture
How will all the concerns swirling around in your thoughts influence you 5 or 10 years from now? Will anybody really care if you purchased a fruit dish for the potluck instead of creating a pie from scratch?

Don't let tiny concerns evolve into huge obstacles.

6. Do something pleasant for someone else
Trying to alleviate the strain for someone else might help you put things in perspective. Think about ways you may be of help to someone going through a tough moment.

Does your buddy who's in the throes of a divorce require a few hours of child care?

Can you bring up groceries for your neighbor who's been sick?

Realizing you have the capacity to make someone's day better might avoid negative thoughts from taking control. It also provides you something useful to concentrate on instead of your never-ending stream of ideas.

7. Recognize automatic negative thoughts (ANTs) (ANTs)
Automatic negative thoughts (ANTs) relate to knee-jerk unpleasant thoughts, generally including fear or anger, you occasionally experience in response to a scenario.

Tackling ANTs
You may recognize and work through your ANTs by keeping a record of your thoughts and actively striving to modify them:

Use a journal to chronicle the circumstance
bringing you anxiety, your emotions, and
the first idea that occurs to you instinctively.
As you dive into specifics, assess why the
scenario is creating these negative feelings.

Break down the feelings you're having and
attempt to determine what you're telling
yourself about the scenario.
Find an alternate to your initial concept.

 For example, instead of leaping right to,
"This is going to be an incredible failure," try
something along the lines of, "I'm honestly
doing my best."

8. Acknowledge your triumphs
When you're in the thick of overthinking,
pause and pull out your notepad or your
favorite note-taking software on your phone.
Jot down five things that have gone
correctly during the previous week and your
part in them.

These don't need to be enormous successes.
Maybe you kept to your coffee budget this
week or cleaned out your vehicle. When you
look at it on paper or on-screen, you could
be shocked at how these tiny things pile up.

If it seems useful, look return to this list
when you find your thoughts swirling.

9. Stay present
Not ready to commit to a meditation
routine? There are lots of other techniques
to anchor oneself in the present moment.

Be here now
Here are a few ideas:

Unplug. Shut off your computer or phone
for a predetermined length of time each day,
and spend that time on a single activity.
Eat thoughtfully. Treat yourself to one of
your favorite dinners. Try to discover the
delight in each mouthful, and truly

concentrate on how the food tastes, smells, and feels in your mouth.
Get outdoors. Take a stroll outdoors, even if it's only a fast loop around the block. Take inventory of everything you see along the journey, including any aromas that float past or noises you hear.

10. Consider other perspectives
Sometimes, quieting your thoughts involves moving outside of your regular viewpoint. How you perceive the world is influenced by your life experiences, attitudes, and assumptions. Imagining things from a new point of view might help you get through some of the noise.

Jot down some of the ideas running around in your brain. Try to analyze how legitimate each one is. For example, maybe you're fretting about an impending vacation because you just know it's going to be a catastrophe. But is that truly what's going to happen? What type of evidence do you have to back that up?

11. Take action
Sometimes, you could go through the same ideas constantly because you aren't taking any tangible activities concerning a given problem.

Can't stop thinking about someone you envy? Instead of letting it destroy your day, let your sentiments help you make better decisions.

The next time you're visited by the green-eyed monster, be proactive and note down methods you can go about accomplishing your objectives. This will pull you out of your brain and redirect your energy into taking concrete measures.

12. Practice self-compassion
Dwelling on previous errors stops you from letting go. If you're beating yourself up over

something you did last week, try focused on self-compassionTrusted Source.

Here are some ideas to get you started:

Take note of a stressful thought.
Pay attention to the emotions and body reactions that occur.
Acknowledge that your emotions are accurate for you in the moment.
Adopt a phrase that speaks to you, such as "May I accept myself as I am" or "I am enough."

13. Embrace your fears
Some things will always be out of your control. Learning how to accept this may go a long way toward limiting overthinking.

Of course, this is easier said than done, and it won't happen quickly. But hunt for little moments where you may tackle the circumstances you regularly worry about. Maybe it's standing up to a pushy co-worker or taking that solitary day trip you've been dreaming about.

14. Ask for assistance
You don't have to do it alone. Seeking outside assistance from a trained therapist may help you acquire new techniques for dealing with your ideas and possibly altering your perspective.

What is rumination?

Has your brain ever been filled with one single idea, or a stream of thoughts, that simply keep repeating... and repeating... and repeating themselves?

The practice of continually thinking about the same ideas, which tend to be gloomy or negative, is termed rumination.

A practice of ruminating may be detrimental to your mental health, since it can prolong or deepen depression as well as impede your capacity to think and process emotions. It may also lead you to feel lonely and may, in truth, drive others away.

What causes ruminating?

People ruminate for a number of reasons. notion that through ruminating, you'll acquire insight into your life or a problem\shaving a history of mental or physical trauma\sfacing continuing

 pressures that can't be handled Ruminating is also typical among those who exhibit particular personality qualities, which include perfectionism, neuroticism, and an obsessive concentration on one's connections with others.

You can have a propensity to overvalue your connections with people so much that you'll make huge personal sacrifices to retain your relationships, even if they're not working for you.

Tips for handling ruminating thoughts
Once you are engaged in a ruminating thought cycle, it might be hard to pull out of it. If you do begin a cycle of such thoughts, it's crucial to interrupt them as fast as possible to avoid them from growing more intense.

As when a ball is going downhill, it's simpler to stop the ruminating thoughts when they initially start rolling and have less speed than after they've accumulated momentum over time.

So, what can you do to stop these obsessive ideas from going through your mind?

Here are 10 strategies to attempt when you begin to have the same idea, or group of thoughts, circling through your head:

1. Distract yourself
When you realize you're starting to
ruminate, finding a distraction can break
your thought cycle. Look about you,
immediately select something else to do,
and don't give it a second thought. Consider:

phoning a friend or family member\sdoing
tasks around your house\swatching a
movie\sdrawing a picture\sreading a
book\swalking around your neighborhood

2. Plan to take action
Instead of repeating the same negative idea
over and over again, take that notion and
form a strategy to take action to solve it.

In your brain, outline each action you need
to do to handle the situation, or write it
down on a piece of paper. Be as precise as
possible and also reasonable with your
expectations.

Doing this will disturb your rumination. It will also assist you go on in the quest to push a bad idea out of your brain once and for all.

3. Take action
Once you've created a plan of action to address your ruminating thoughts, take one tiny move to address the problem. Refer to the strategy you prepared to tackle the issue you've been stressing about.

Move ahead with each step carefully and progressively until your mind is set at peace.

4. Question your thoughts
We typically ruminate when we believe we've made a significant mistake or when something awful has occurred to us that we feel responsible for.

If you start ruminating on a worrisome concept, consider putting your recurring thought in context.

Thinking more about how your worrying notion could not be true may help you stop ruminating since you recognize the thought makes little sense.

5. Readjust your life's objectives
Perfectionism and unrealistic goal setting may lead to rumination. If you establish objectives that are unreasonable, you may start to concentrate on why and how you haven't attained a goal, or what you should have done to accomplish it.

Setting more realistic objectives that you're capable of accomplishing may lessen the hazards of overthinking your own activities.

6. Work on increasing your self-esteem
Many persons who ruminate report challenges with self-esteem. In fact, loss of self-esteem might be connected with greater ruminating. It's also been connected with higher risk of depression.

Enhancement of self-esteem can be accomplished in many ways. For instance, expanding on current abilities may contribute to a feeling of mastery, which can increase self-esteem.

Some persons may opt to focus on the strengthening of self-esteem in psychotherapy. As you boost your self-esteem, self-efficacy may also be strengthened. You may notice that you're better able to regulate ruminating.

7. Try meditation
Meditating helps lessen ruminating since it entails cleansing your thoughts to get at an emotionally peaceful state.

When you find yourself with a repeated cycle of ideas in your head, seek out a calm spot. Sit down, breathe deeply, and focus on nothing but breathing.

8. Understand your triggers
Each time you find yourself ruminating, make a mental note of the scenario you're in.

This includes where you are, what time of day it is, who's around you (if anybody), and what you've been doing that day.

Developing ways to avoid or manage these triggers can reduce your rumination.

9. Talk to a buddy
Ruminating thoughts might make you feel alone. Talking about your ideas with a buddy who can give an outside viewpoint may help stop the loop.

Be careful to chat with a buddy who can offer you that perspective rather than ruminate with you.

10. Try treatment

If your ruminating thoughts are taking over your life, you may want to seek counselling. A therapist can help you determine why you're ruminating and how to address the issues at their root.

Lifestyle changes
If you're a long-time ruminator who wishes to put a stop to your recurring negative thoughts, here are some easy adjustments you can make to your life that can help achieve exactly that:

Be proactive in trying to solve your problems. First identify difficulties in your life and then start taking activities to remedy your problems, one step at a time Set your own expectations.

Negative ruminating thoughts might come in when we doubt our self-worth. Praise yourself for your triumphs and forgive yourself for your faults. Constantly concentrate on increasing your self-esteem by taking care of yourself and doing activities you like and succeed at.

Create a support system. Having friends and family members, and maybe even a therapist, any of whom you can depend on for support when something goes wrong or when you're having a difficult day, is extremely vital.

These special people may distract you from your ruminating thoughts and are also likely to boost your self-esteem.

It is possible to stop ruminating
If you're a ruminator, it's crucial to know certain methods that may enable you to halt your thinking cycle in its tracks before it spirals out of hand.

It's also crucial to be proactive and take actions to avoid yourself from ruminating in the first place.

With awareness and certain lifestyle modifications, it's possible to liberate yourself from ruminating ideas. If you discover that you're unable to apply these methods to ease your ruminating, you may consider contacting a mental health professional for support.

Chapter 2

Learn how to love yourself

Learn How to Self-love
Self-love is a word that is regularly tossed about even in casual speech. You have likely heard:

"You need to love yourself more."

"Why don't you love yourself?"

"You can't love someone else if you don't love yourself first."

Sayings like these are tiresome when it comes to providing people recommendations on how to have a more full life, methods to have more confidence, ways to be more successful, or ways to feel anything other than what they are experiencing.

But when we speak about self-love in times such as these, do we genuinely grasp what we are talking about?

Let's go a bit more into this holy and delicate issue of how to self-love.

What is Self-love?
Self-love is not only a condition of feeling wonderful; it is an activity. Self-love is a decision. It is a style of connecting to oneself that comprises being understanding of your faults, understanding your losses, and being able to successfully speak with yourself about life without harshly criticizing or punishing yourself.

Research has revealed that knowing how to self-love is connected with:

Less anxiety and sadness
Better recovery from stress\sAn generally more happy attitude on life\sBetter commitment to good behavior adjustments In summary, self-love is how you regard yourself and how you treat yourself.

Why is Self-Love Important?
Learning how to self-love is vital to living happier and healthier in all parts of your life. It determines who you chose to be your spouse for life, the image you present at work, how you do your job, the way you rear your children, the way you connect with others around you, and the way you deal with the issues in your life.

Why You Might Be Lacking Self-Love
Low self-esteem or lack of self-love is something that might be acquired in infancy

and persist through to maturity. Or, it is
something that might reveal itself primarily
in maturity.

Earlier sexual activity
Alcohol and drug abuse
Self-harm
Eating disorders

You can be lacking self-love for several
causes or behaviors, as described above. It
might be due to the acts of others around
you, because of a painful incident in your
life, because you lacked a strong model of
self-love, or simply because of a style of
thinking that you intrinsically practice.

But, one key thing to remember is that poor
self-esteem owing to a lack of self-love is not
an exact representation of reality, but a
reflection of your view on reality.

Tips to Learn How to Self-Love

While self-love is not always natural, it may be taught. Here are some helpful pointers on how to self-love today:

Recognize How You Are Feeling

You've undoubtedly heard the cliché adage that "the first step to addressing a problem is recognizing that you have one." Well, one of the first stages of learning how to self-love is kind of similar — it is being aware of oneself.

We all experience a range of emotions during our lives — grief, rage, frustration, loneliness, happiness, and more.

When something seems amiss, it is crucial to take a minute to notice how you are feeling at that time and why.

Why are you sad? Why are you angry? Why are you happy?

In self-love, you must be conscious so that you may begin to transform any negative state that is associated with those sentiments.

Accept How You Are Feeling

While there is nothing wrong with experiencing any of the emotions we discussed or others, it is crucial that once you acknowledge your feelings you can embrace them.

Whether you choose to feel it or not, the sensation is there. Take a time to halt and dwell on that emotion.

Now, scan your body to see where you feel it.

Think About Your Feelings from an Outsider's Perspective

How would you feel if you witnessed a loved one experience the sensation you are experiencing at that moment? Then, think about how you may urge them to continue.

What is interesting about life and our brains is that we treat ourselves radically differently than we treat others. While we may attempt to push good conduct on our friend or family member experiencing a bad mood, we would beat ourselves up for feeling this way.

View this issue with a compassionate eye and be nice to yourself. Love yourself in that moment and all ones.

Forgive Yourself

This self-love suggestion truly has two parts to it:

First, consider what it will take to forgive yourself for whatever the issue is.

Second, make a deliberate choice to forgive yourself.

We may be so harsh on ourselves sometimes, but it is crucial to give ourselves a break. You might be your own worst enemy at times.

When you believe you have made a mistake, decide what action you can take to make it right in your own eyes. Then, utilize self-talk to urge yourself to take that step toward forgiveness.

Say No to Others

Sometimes exercising self-love isn't only about speaking respectfully to ourselves while we are experiencing particular emotions. It may also be about taking care of oneself while others are present.

Set limits. Make time for yourself. It is appropriate to tell somebody "no" if you believe that you need to. Love yourself enough to make the proper choice for yourself, not for anybody else.

Self-love is a constant activity, a continuous process, and a continuous decision. You should continuously be investing in yourself by focusing on doing activities that encourage self-love.

Accept Help

One approach to consistently guarantee you are focused on how to self-love and putting recommendations like these into practice is to consider visiting a psychologist often for help.

Self-love is crucial to your entire well-being. Invest in your self – y\sKnow what you seek in a relationship.

Chapter 3

Knowing when you meet toxic people

What Is a Toxic Person?

Signs of a Toxic Person
Dealing With Toxic People
What Is a Toxic Person?

If you know someone who's tough and generates a lot of tension in your life, you may be dealing with a toxic person. These individuals may produce loads of tension and unhappiness for you and others, not to mention emotional or even bodily suffering.

A toxic person is somebody whose conduct contributes negativity and stress to your life. Many times, toxic individuals are struggling with their worries and traumas. To achieve this, they behave in ways that don't portray them in the greatest light and frequently offend others along the way.

Toxicity in persons isn't regarded as a mental disease. But there might be underlying mental disorders that drive someone to behave in poisonous ways, like a personality disorder.

Here are some warning indicators to look out for if you believe you're dealing with a toxic person:

You feel like you're being manipulated into something you don't want to do.

You're continually perplexed by the person's actions.

You feel like you deserve an apology that never comes.

You constantly have to justify yourself to this individual.

You never feel entirely comfortable with them.

You frequently feel horrible about yourself in their company.

If you've had these sensations around someone, they may be poisonous. If you consistently experience such sentiments, you may wish to modify the connection or terminate the relationship.

Signs of a Toxic Person
Just as there are signals you're around a toxic person because of how the person makes you feel, there are signs visible in the person that indicate their toxicity.

The most prevalent indicators include:

Inconsistency

Part of being human is having ups and downs, good times, and bad. But a toxic person is rarely consistent. Their behavior is erratic. They don't follow through on their commitments or promises. You never know what they're going to do next. Such inconsistency is incredibly challenging when you're trying to be there for someone. They might be thrilled with you one minute, writing you off the next.

www.ingramcontent.com/pod-product-compliance
Lightning Source LLC
Chambersburg PA
CBHW070725160726
48003CB00006BA/2385